DIGITAL SAFETY SMARTS

# DEALING WITH
# ONLINE BULLIES

Katie Clark

Lerner Publications ◆ Minneapolis

**Dedicated to my loves, always.**



Lerner Publications Company
An imprint of Lerner Publishing Group, Inc.
241 First Avenue North
Minneapolis, MN 55401 USA

For reading levels and more information, look up this title at www.lernerbooks.com.

Main body text set in Aptifer Sans LT Pro
Typeface provided by Linotype.

**Library of Congress Cataloging-in-Publication Data**

Names: Clark, Katie, 1983–author.
Title: Dealing with online bullies / Katie Clark.
Description: Minneapolis : Lerner Publications, [2026] | Series: Digital safety smarts (alternator books) | Includes bibliographical references and index. | Audience: Ages 8–12 | Audience: Grades 4–6 | Summary: "Any online avatar could be hiding a cyberbully. Readers discover how to identify harmful language and behavior online, and what to do about it. This includes speaking up about bullies, blocking them, and more"—Provided by publisher.
Identifiers: LCCN 2024050404 (print) | LCCN 2024050405 (ebook) | ISBN 9798765668252 (library binding) | ISBN 9798765683842 (paperback) | ISBN 9798765676417 (epub)
Subjects: LCSH: Cyberbullying—Juvenile literature. | Cyberbullying—Prevention—Juvenile literature.
Classification: LCC HV6773.15.C92 C59 2026 (print) | LCC HV6773.15.C92 (ebook) | DDC 302.34/3028546—dc23/eng/20250115

LC record available at https://lccn.loc.gov/2024050404
LC ebook record available at https://lccn.loc.gov/2024050405

Manufactured in the United States of America
1 – CG – 7/15/25

# TABLE OF CONTENTS

# MORE THAN TRASH TALK

Chris zapped the last alien spacecraft and cheered. He'd won! It had been a long day at school, and now he was winding down in his bedroom with an online video game.

He heard a ping in his headset. He had a message from another gamer.

"Can I join your team?" the message said.

Chris tapped on the gamer's name. The kid had bad stats, and Chris laughed. He typed his reply.

"No way, you're like the worst player I've ever seen!"

When the next game started, the other gamer ended up on the opposite team. Chris sent him another message.

"I don't know why you're trying," he said. "You stink!"

A few minutes later, he sent another message. "Just give up now. You're the worst!"

Online gaming often involves trash talk, but gamers need to be careful that it doesn't turn into bullying.

Just then, his grandpa opened the door. "What's up, Chris?" Grandpa asked.

"Playing some games," Chris said.

His grandfather looked over his shoulder.

When Grandpa saw what Chris had typed, he frowned. "Who are these messages to?"

"That's no one," Chris said. "I forgot to minimize the message screen."

Grandpa shook his head. "You shouldn't be talking to anyone like that. Trash talk during a game is one thing, but this is more than trash talk. You don't have a reason to be so mean to someone."

Chris felt heat rise in his cheeks. "Yes, sir," he said. "I won't do it again."

# CHAPTER ONE

# UNDERSTANDING CYBERBULLYING

Have you ever heard of a cyberbully? A cyberbully is someone who targets people online with hurtful, harassing messages. They try to embarrass or trick their target. Sometimes they're trying to steal personal data, while other times they're simply being cruel.

It is important to know that cyberbullies are often victims of being bullied themselves. They may bully others as a type of revenge for the bullying they've experienced. They might also bully others because of mental health issues or even jealousy.

Do you think Chris was being a cyberbully in his online game? His grandpa seemed to think so! Cyberbullying can happen anywhere online. It might happen on social media or in online games, emails, or text groups.

## What Makes Someone a Cyberbully?

Cyberbullying comes in many forms. It might include name-calling or spreading rumors about someone.

Sometimes it can be funny to poke fun at or discuss rumors about other people. Many people call this teasing. However, when the name-calling and rumors keep going, and

People online who use mean and hurtful language to make someone feel bad are cyberbullies.

it embarrasses the person who is being talked about, it has probably gone too far.

How can you tell the difference between teasing and bullying? When does it cross the line between having a little fun and being cruel?

Look for certain clues. For example, if someone asks you to stop saying something they feel is mean or hurtful, the best thing to do is stop. If you don't, you are acting like a bully. Reference the handy chart on the next page for tips on how to tell the difference between teasing and bullying.

## How Cyberbullying Affects Others

Cyberbullying can be a huge deal. No one likes a bully! Though kids might laugh with them for a little while, the bully

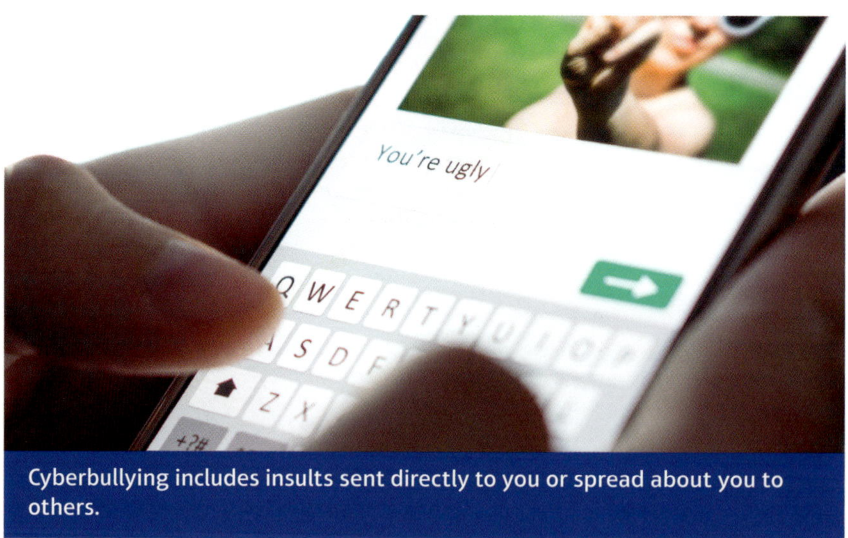


Cyberbullying includes insults sent directly to you or spread about you to others.

| TEASING | BULLYING |
| --- | --- |
| Can include an argument between friends | Can happen anywhere |
| Good-natured and playful | Intentional—meant to cause distress |
| Equal—not ganging up on one person | Done by someone who wants to feel powerful |
| Not repeated | Repeated over and over |
| They'd stop if you asked them to | Done with the intention of intimidating—looking for control through fear |

will soon find out that no one trusts them. They will probably find themselves with very few friends.

Besides that, being bullied can have big emotional and mental impacts on the victim. Getting bullied can cause a person to lose self-confidence, get poor grades, hide away, develop depression or anxiety, or perform self-harm.

Cyberbullying is intentional behavior meant to cause harm.

# The Cyberbullying Process: How it Happens

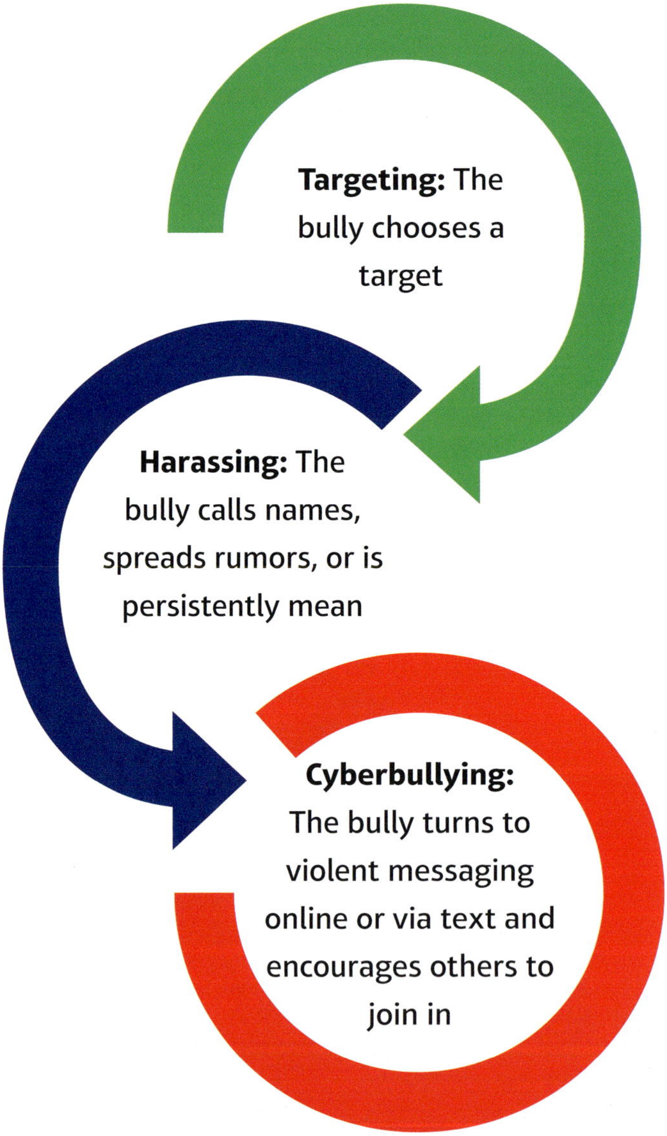

Ask yourself: do you want to be the kind of person who bullies someone else? Sometimes we may not intend to become a cyberbully, but it can be easy to slip into bad habits when we're online. This is because when we aren't looking at someone face to face, we might feel braver to say mean or cruel things. It is like hiding behind our screens, thinking no one can see our bad behavior.

Research shows us that one out of five kids between the ages of nine and twelve has been involved with cyberbullying. The best thing you can do is to not join in! If you see signs that you are being a cyberbully, do what Chris did and stop. If someone you know is being a cyberbully, encourage them to stop their actions. You should also tell a trusted adult.

## TIP TO REMEMBER

**Online words can hurt just as much as in-person words. Always think before you send or post!**

# CHAPTER TWO

# WHAT TO DO

Cyberbullying can be scary, especially when someone is harassing you and won't stop. Remember that the bully is just trying to get a reaction out of you, and the things they're saying about you aren't true. If you are experiencing cyberbullying, there are steps you can take to protect yourself.

# How to Deal with a Cyberbully

First of all, don't respond or retaliate when someone is bullying you online. This will usually encourage the bully to act out even more.

Instead, save proof of the bullying and protect yourself. To do this, take screenshots or save the messages as evidence so you can get proper help. Once you have saved the proof, you will want to block the bully. Do this by clicking on their profile and then selecting the option to block or report the user.

## Talk to a Trusted Adult

The next step is to tell a trusted adult. An adult will know if cyberbullying has gone too far and if action needs to be taken

The constant harassment from an online bully can be tough to deal with, but don't give the bully what they want. Never reply!

against the bully. They can also help you understand how to handle the problem.

Who should you tell? A parent or guardian is usually a good place to start. Your teacher or school counselor are other great options. If you are uncomfortable with these options, try confiding in a friend so someone knows what's going on with you in case you need help.

Whether it's an adult or a friend, the most important thing to remember is that you should always tell someone. Sometimes bullies warn their victims to tell no one, but don't listen to the bully! Talk to someone about it instead.

Don't let a bully tell you what to do. No matter what they say, tell a trusted adult.

# Nearly half of surveyed teens report having experienced cyberbullying

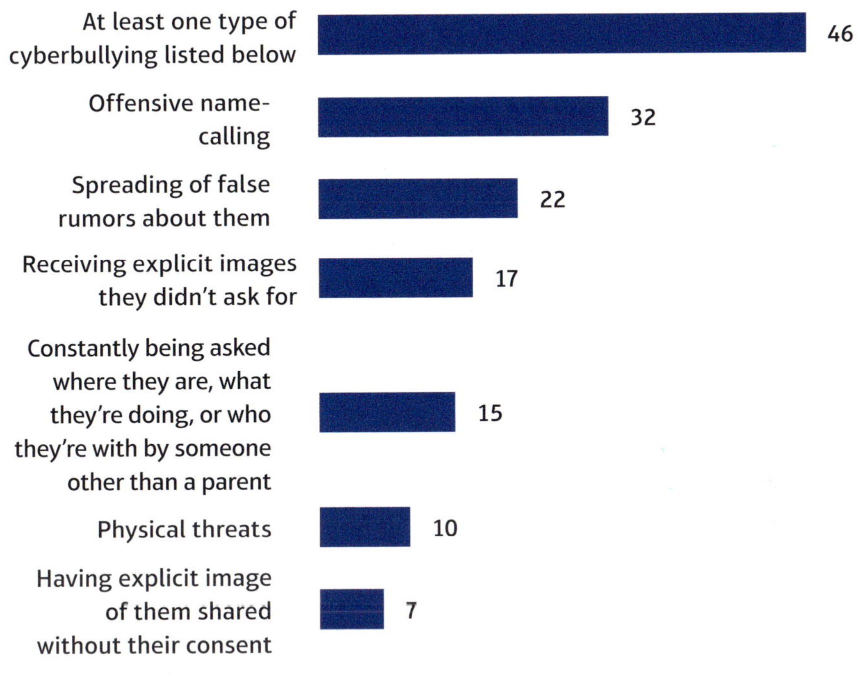


Note: Teens are those ages 13 to 17. Those who did not give an answer are not shown.
Source: Survey conducted April 14-May 4, 2022.
Teens and Cyberbullying 2022
PEW RESEARCH CENTER

Getting called nasty names is the most common issue reported by cyberbullied teens.

# Preventing Cyberbullying

There are steps you can take to help keep yourself safe online. Adjust your privacy settings to keep out the people you don't trust. You can do this by going into the "settings" feature on the game, app, or social media platform you're using. Choose the "private" option, or the one that only lets your friends see your activity.

You should also avoid sharing personal information online. Don't share the name of the city where you live, the school you attend, or your phone number with strangers. When in doubt, ask a trusted adult before sharing!

## NOT YOUR FAULT

**Cyberbullying can happen to anyone. It's never your fault if someone is mean to you online.**

Cyberbullying can be upsetting in many ways. Don't go through it alone.

# CHAPTER THREE

# HELPING OTHERS

Getting bullied is no fun. This is true whether the bullying is online or offline. It can also be tough to have friends who are getting bullied. Would you know if your friend was a cyberbully's target?

# Recognizing the Signs of Bullying

If your friend is being cyberbullied, there could be signs. They might start acting differently by becoming withdrawn, quiet, or grumpy. They might start avoiding online activities. This could mean they drop off social media, quit online gaming, or get defensive when you ask about their absence from these activities.

It is important to know that just because a friend is grouchy doesn't automatically mean they are being cyberbullied. However, if they are also withdrawing from online activity, cyberbullying could be a reason.

If a friend is not acting like themselves and seems more sad or angry, online bullying is a possible cause.

## Online Hero

Anna Holcombe is a teen from Georgia who learned about cyberbullying during a class project. She was inspired to make a difference in this area. She said, "Automatically, I felt the need to stand up for these children and teens." Anna travels around the country and speaks at events to teach people about bullying and how to stop it. She encourages kids, teens, and adults to take a step toward leadership and put a stop to bullying!

# Supporting a Friend

If you suspect your friend is being cyberbullied, talk it out with them. Encourage them to save evidence of the bullying and then block the bully. You can also urge them to talk to an adult.

It's best to never take matters into your own hands. Don't confront the bully. Instead, speak to a trusted adult who can help find a solution.

# When Cyberbullying is Happening

You might have witnessed cyberbullying online before. Sometimes, you might spot it in a texting group when people are making fun of someone else. It might also happen on social media.

If you witness this type of behavior, don't join in. Decide for yourself that you won't be part of the problem!

Never join in if you witness bullying in person or online.

# Steps to Support a Friend

 Pay attention to the way your friend is acting

 Tell an adult what is happening

 Block the cyberbullies

 Put a stop to bullying

If you see online bullying happening, stand up to the bully and see if their keyboard courage goes away.

You can also stand up for others by changing the tone of the conversation. Say something positive. You could also change the subject entirely.

Taking a stand in this way might feel scary. You might worry that you'll be the bully's next target.

However, you might be surprised instead. Online bullies rely on keyboard courage. This means that they only dare to be mean to people online where they are hidden behind their keyboard. Also, others will take notice that you're standing up for what is right. This type of positivity can spread quickly! If you do find yourself getting picked on for taking a stand, quietly leave the conversation. Don't stick around!

# CHAPTER FOUR

# POSITIVE ONLINE COMMUNITY

With all the talk about bullying, it is just as important to talk about being kind. You will most likely find that in all areas of your life, kindness is king!

# Use the Internet for Good

The internet can be an amazing place. Can you imagine a world where you could not search for fun facts in an instant or look up dates for upcoming events?

We can add to the awesomeness of the internet by making sure we are being kind online. We should always support our friends online! Do this by sharing fun and inspiring messages and pictures, and by interacting positively with others. When playing a multiplayer game, never send bullying messages, and keep an upbeat outlook.

It's easy to find ways to use the internet for good. You could join or support worthy causes, share positive messages, or be kind to others on social media.

# Handle Conflicts the Right Way

When a problem does pop up, don't panic. Remember that everyone thinks differently. What might seem right to you may feel different to someone in a different situation. Diversity of experiences and opinions can be a wonderful thing!

The more people that speak out against online bullying, the more likely it is that bullies will get the message.

If disagreements arise, always stay calm. We should respect each other even when we disagree. It's good to avoid negative arguments. If you can't agree with someone, it can be best to stop talking about the subject for a little while.

## Spreading Awareness

The internet is also a great place to spread awareness about cyberbullying. You can speak out against cyberbullying and become a champion for spreading kindness. You can also encourage your friends to do the same thing. There is power in numbers!

Knowing how to avoid online bullies will make the internet a better experience for you and your friends.

# Make a Difference!

Remember, it is important to steer clear of cyberbullies. It is also important to never become one yourself!

If you encounter cyberbullying, save the messages or take screenshots as proof. Then report and block the user.

Never share personal information with strangers, and keep your profiles private. This will help protect you!

If you suspect a friend is being bullied, speak up. Ask them if they are all right. If they need help, you can be a good friend by directing them to an adult who can help them.

Doing these things will help create a better online experience for everyone!

If you take appropriate action when facing online bullies, it will help you to get rid of them for good.

Dealing with online bullying is no fun—staying kind and connected makes using mobile devices a positive experience for everyone!

# GLOSSARY

**awareness:** knowledge and understanding about something

**cyberbully:** a person who posts mean-spirited messages online

**disagreement:** not agreeing with someone

**diversity:** being made up of different things

**harass:** to create a situation that brings worry, exhaustion, or hostility

**impact:** to have a big effect on something or someone

**personal information:** private details that relate to a specific person

**privacy setting:** online tools that help limit access to personal information

**retaliate:** to treat someone in the same way they have treated you

**self-harm:** hurting oneself as a way to deal with or distract from intense emotions

**victim:** a person that is bullied, fooled, or harmed by another

# LEARN MORE


Clark, Katie. *Playing Online Games.* Minneapolis: Lerner Publications, 2026.

Geiser, Dagmar. *How Can I Be Safe Online? Learning How to Behave and Protect Myself on the Internet.* Sky Pony Press. 2025.

Harasymiw, Therese. *You Can Help Stop Bullying!* New York: Powerkids, 2021.

KidsHealth: Dealing with Bullies
https://kidshealth.org/en/kids/bullies.html

*National Geographic Kids:* Six helpful Tips on How to Stop Bullying
https://www.natgeokids.com/uk/kids-club/cool-kids/general-kids
-club/stop-bullying/

Roberts, Jillian. *On the Internet: Our First Talk About Online Safety.* Victoria, Canada: Orca Books Publishing. 2022.

StopBullying.gov: What Kids Can Do
https://www.stopbullying.gov/kids/what-you-can-do

UNICEF: Cyberbullying
https://www.unicef.org/end-violence/how-to-stop-cyberbullying

# INDEX



# PHOTO ACKNOWLEDGMENTS


Image credits: DC Studio/Shutterstock, p. 5; SrideeStudio/Shutterstock, p. 7; Tero Vesalainen/Shutterstock, p. 8; Halfpoint/Shutterstock, p. 9; CLS Digital Arts/Shutterstock, p. 11; AnnaStills/Shutterstock, p. 13; DimaBerlin/Shutterstock, pp. 14, 16; SpeedKingz/Shutterstock, p.17; Antonio Guillem/Shutterstock, p. 19; Lightfield Studios/Shutterstock, p. 21; Ariya J/Shutterstock, p. 23; Jevanto Productions/Shutterstock, p. 25; PeopleImages.com - Yuri A/Shutterstock, p. 26; TommyStockProject/Shutterstock p. 27; Rawpixel.com/Shutterstock, p. 28; Xavier Lorenzo/Shutterstock, p. 29; Just dance/Shutterstock, p. 31. Cover image: Monkey Business Images/Shutterstock.